SEASONS OF FUN: SUMMER

by Finley Fraser

Consultant: Beth Gambro
Reading Specialist, Yorkville, Illinois

Minneapolis, Minnesota

Teaching Tips

Before Reading

- Look at the cover of the book. Discuss the picture and the title.
- Ask readers to brainstorm a list of what they already know about summer weather. What can they expect to see in the book?
- Go on a picture walk, looking through the pictures to discuss vocabulary and make predictions about the text.

During Reading

- Read for purpose. Encourage readers to think about the weather they might see in the summer as they are reading.
- Ask readers to look for the details of the book. What kinds of weather are included?
- If readers encounter an unknown word, ask them to look at the sounds in the word. Then, ask them to look at the rest of the page. Are there any clues to help them understand?

After Reading

- Encourage readers to pick a buddy and reread the book together.
- Ask readers to name three types of weather from the book that can happen during summer. Go back and find the pages that tell about each type.
- Ask readers to write or draw something they learned about summer weather.

Credits:
Cover and title page, © Firn/Shutterstock; 3, © New Africa/Shutterstock; 5, © Rawpixel.com/Shutterstock; 6–7, © SerrNovik/iStock; 9, © Rido/Shutterstock; 10–11, © kate_sept2004/iStock; 12–13, © Yulia_B/Shutterstock; 14–15, © mdesigner125/iStock; 17, © PeopleImages/iStock; 18–19, © TomasSereda/iStock; 21, © KieferPix/Shutterstock; 22 background, © Anna.Sven/Shutterstock; 22, © koblizeek/Shutterstock, © spline_x/Shutterstock, © ifong/Shutterstock, and © AbraSa/Shutterstock; 23TL, © Slavica/iStock; 23TM, © Andrey Bocharov/Shutterstock; 23TR, © petrograd99/iStock; 23B, © EvgeniiAnd/iStock; and 23BR, © SusanneSchulz/iStock.

Library of Congress Cataloging-in-Publication Data

Names: Fraser, Finley, 1972- author.
Title: Summer weather / by Finley Fraser.
Description: Minneapolis, Minnesota : Bearport Publishing [2023] | Series: Seasons of fun: Summer | Includes bibliographical references and index.
Identifiers: LCCN 2022025646 (print) | LCCN 2022025647 (ebook) | ISBN 9798885093316 (library binding) | ISBN 9798885094535 (paperback) | ISBN 9798885095686 (ebook)
Subjects: LCSH: Weather--Juvenile literature. | Summer--Juvenile literature. | Meteorology--Juvenile literature.
Classification: LCC QC981.3 .F73 2023 (print) | LCC QC981.3 (ebook) | DDC 398/.363--dc23
LC record available at https://lccn.loc.gov/2022025646
LC ebook record available at https://lccn.loc.gov/2022025647

Copyright ©2023 Bearport Publishing Company. All rights reserved. No part of this publication may be reproduced in whole or in part, stored in any retrieval system, or transmitted in any form or by any means, electronic, mechanical, photocopying, recording, or otherwise, without written permission from the publisher.

For more information, write to Bearport Publishing, 5357 Penn Avenue South, Minneapolis, MN 55419.

Contents

Fun in the Summer Sun 4

Colorful Rainbows 22

Glossary 23

Index 24

Read More 24

Learn More Online..................... 24

About the Author 24

Fun in the Summer Sun

It is time for summer fun!

Many places are sunny and hot in the summer.

What is the weather like today?

The sun rises early in the morning.

The sky is blue.

It is going to be a hot day.

We put on shorts and T-shirts.

Let's go outside!

First, we need to put on **sunscreen**.

We want to stay safe in the sun!

We drink water as we play outside.

It is good to take breaks in the **shade**, too.

These things help us keep cool.

My brother finds shapes in the clouds.

That one looks like a duck!

Soon, gray clouds start to fill the sky.

The sky gets darker.

It starts to rain.

We see **lightning**.

It is time to go inside!

Sometimes, there are bad storms in the summer.

The rain starts to fall harder.

We hear **thunder**.

Boom!

I like to watch summer storms from the window.

Soon, it stops raining.

The sun comes out.

There is a **rainbow** in the sky.

It is so pretty!

The sun is up for a long time in the summer!

When it gets dark, it is almost time for bed.

There are plenty of hot days ahead.

We love summer weather!

Colorful Rainbows

You might see a rainbow after rain! How do rainbows form?

1. Sunlight goes through raindrops.
2. Then, the raindrops bend the light.
3. This makes us see many colors curved high in the sky.

Light

Glossary

lightning a flash of light that comes from a storm

rainbow a curve with many colors in the sky

shade a place away from the sun

sunscreen a cream that goes on skin to keep you safe from the sun

thunder a loud sound that comes from storms

Index

hot 4, 6, 20
lightning 14
play 10
rain 14, 16, 18, 22
rainbow 18, 22
shade 10
sunscreen 8
thunder 16

Read More

Gardner, Jane P. *Rainbows (Amazing Sights in the Sky).* Minneapolis: Jump!, 2021.

Rotner, Shelley. *Hello Summer! (Hello Seasons!).* New York: Holiday House, 2019.

Learn More Online

1. Go to **www.factsurfer.com** or scan the QR code below.
2. Enter "**Summer Weather**" into the search box.
3. Click on the cover of this book to see a list of websites.

About the Author

Finley Fraser is a writer living in Portland, Maine. In the summer he complains about the heat. Then, he takes it all back when winter comes.